A father to the fatherless,
a defender of widows,
is God in His holy dwelling.

Psalm 68:5

You are my treasure,
God set you apart.
I've always carried you
inside of my heart.

Here is a tale of
wonder and glee.
Tis the story of how
you and I became WE.

Once upon a time,
I asked God for a child.
He listened with love,
then so brightly He smiled.

Our special family, woven together by hand. Mysterious works, I hope to one day understand.

Even when you couldn't see me
I've always been there.
Covering you with blankets of love,
and wrapping you in prayer.

I didn't feel your kicks
or have pains nor prickles.
When God placed you in my heart
it felt more like tickles!

Overjoyed! My body began glowing,
rather than DNA,

LOVE began flowing!

There was no baby-bump
like many moms-to-be.
Instead I wore a smile so big
the whole world could see!

The cravings they came
not for sour or sweet.
I longed for the day
you and I would finally meet!

Instead of a black and white, blurry ultrasound. I saw you crystal clear, wearing courage as a crown.

More glorious than the vast starry night skies,
I cherish the moment I first looked into your eyes.

Like a long awaited spring now in full bloom.
The sight of you was like flowers,
with the sweetest perfume.

Through the magic of fairytales, and lands of make-believe, memories, laughter, and life lessons we'll weave.

As we tiptoe into dawn's shiny new day, I watch in amazement as you learn and you play.

Each morning brings excitement, on adventures we'll go! Now until forever, together we'll grow.

When you see a waterfall
in the sunbeam,
think of my love as
a never ending stream.

Let's Pray Together

God, thank You for adoption, for knitting families together, and for loving us. Thank You for entrusting us with these beautiful children. Please uplift their hearts, be close to them, and mend any sorrows You find in the depths of their spirits.

Let them be filled with JOY!

Let these little ones drift away to sleep knowing they are chosen, purposefully created, and forever loved. Give us all peace knowing You are the Creator of families, and You have always carried us in your heart.

Amen.

About the Author

Sarah Lutz is called to share meaningful stories with adopted children. She assures them of God's beautiful plans for their lives, sparks excitement for their bright future, and reinforces how very loved they are.

Inspiration for this book came when her daughter asked to pretend to come from Sarah's tummy. God gave Sarah perfect words for that moment, "You were carried in my heart. I've always loved you. I've always wanted you, and I've always prayed for you. Most mommies only have to wait 9-months – I had to wait YEARS to meet you!" Her daughter's eyes filled with tears accompanied by a big smile and hugs and kisses.

Sarah understands that many adopted children long to hear about the day they were born, and oh what a magical story being Carried in my Heart is! Sarah's deepest wish is that you use her books to create precious memories with your children.

Written with LOVE

Matt, Chloe, Wyatt, and Finnessy,
you are my everything.

My love for you is so BIG a zillion-trillion books wouldn't be enough to describe how much love my heart carries for you.

A special thanks to my daughter Chloe Lutz for helping with pictures and words. I love you Chlo-bear!

♡
Mom

Made in the USA
Coppell, TX
06 May 2023